Horse Trail Riding Safety and Etiquette

Tips and Advice for Safe and Fun Trail Riding

Kim Baker

Copyright © 2012 Kim Baker, Kimberly AJ Baker, and Kim AJ Baker, Inc.

All rights reserved.

ISBN-10: 1477663983
ISBN-13: 978-1477663981

DEDICATION

To Night, for all the wonderful trail rides we have done together.

CONTENTS

	Acknowledgments	i
1	Safety & Etiquette	1
2	Check List	3
3	Bad Weather	6
4	Trailer Check List	9
5	Keeping Your Horse Cool in Hot Weather	11
6	How to Tell if Your Horse is Overheated	14
7	Pre-Ride Checklist	16
8	Hunting Season	18
9	Dogs	21
10	Bikes	23
11	Summary	26

ACKNOWLEDGMENTS

Cover Photo by Susan Muscutt. I would like to thank my editor Ellen Haight for the wonderful work she does. I would like to thank my ex-husband for his support and assistance in all things horse related despite his reluctance. Love and light for my family, mentors and friends. And most of all for the horses – the master teachers!

1 SAFETY & ETIQUETTE

Trail riding is fun and a great way to explore different parts of the countryside and nature. To ensure you have safe and happy ride, take note of the following tips:

Horse Gear – a properly fitting saddle is a must, as are a halter and lead rope. Saddle bags, breast collar, rear cinch or crupper, hoof boot, and hoof pick are important items as well.

Safety Gear – helmet, cell phone, first aid kit (horse and human), pocket knife or multiple-purpose tool, rain gear, water and food, compass/map/GPS, duct tape and baling twine are all essential items to have on the trail. Note: keep the most important items on your person in a small pack in case you and your horse get separated.

Trail Hazards – make sure you and your horse are prepared to handle the unexpected out on the trail before you leave the arena. Don't ride over footing/areas where you cannot see the bottom and or depth (e.g., river, bogs, underbrush, etc.). Make sure you can mount and dismount your horse from both sides (left and right) – this is important when you're on a steep hill.

Buddy Rule – ride with a friend or in a group. If you must go out by yourself, make sure you tell someone where you are going and how long you think you'll be gone.

Trail Etiquette – experienced riders/horses should lead and bring up the rear of a group. Keep the pace according to the least experienced rider/horse. Communicate in your group and ask permission from all riders to pick up the pace. If you feel uncomfortable, it is ok to get off your horse and lead him or her through/over an obstacle – just make sure you've done your groundwork at home so your horse doesn't run you over.

Inform Others with Color Codes – tie a ribbon of specific color into your horse's tail to inform those in your group and others out on the trails.
Red = kicker
Yellow = stallion
Green = young/inexperienced horse and/or rider.
White = vision impairment of horse and/or rider.

Wildlife – The safest strategy is to stay on your horse and either go around or allow the wildlife to pass you. Members of the ungulate (deer) family will most likely run away from you and your horse. Be cautious around temperamental animals like moose and bear; stay on your horse and do your best to make a wide berth around them. Predators like mountain lions are the most dangerous. <u>Do not</u> get off your horse. Make a lot of loud noise and try to scare the animal off. If you and your horse run, the mountain lion's predator instinct will be triggered and it will likely chase you.

Emergencies – stay calm! Remember to take deep breaths. Designate one rider to go back to get help. Clear the area, keep a level head and assess what needs to be done until help arrives.

2 CHECK LIST

Day Trip – Close to Home

- ✓ Helmet
- ✓ First Aid Kit – Human and Horse
- ✓ Water
- ✓ Food
- ✓ Cell Phone
- ✓ All purpose knife (Leatherman/Swiss Army Knife)
- ✓ Wind/Waterproof jacket
- ✓ Layered clothing
- ✓ Whistle
- ✓ Horse Boot

> **Day Trip – Away from Home**
>
> - ✓ Helmet
> - ✓ First Aid Kit – Human and Horse
> - ✓ Water
> - ✓ Food
> - ✓ Cell Phone
> - ✓ All purpose knife (Leatherman/Swiss Army Knife)
> - ✓ Wind/Waterproof jacket
> - ✓ Layered clothing
> - ✓ Compass
> - ✓ Emergency/Space Blanket
> - ✓ Matches/Flint
> - ✓ Glow sticks
> - ✓ Kleenex tissues
> - ✓ Whistle
> - ✓ Horse Boot
> - ✓ Leather Straps/Strings
> - ✓ Flashlight
> - ✓ Duct Tape

Additional items to consider:

- Extra batteries for flashlight
- Large plastic trash bag (extra rain poncho, make shift lean too, etc.)
- Packaged drink
- Additional food supply that won't melt
- Travel sized tubes/bottles of:
    - sun block
    - lip balm
    - waterproof insect repellent
    - petroleum jelly or Destin for chafing and abrasions
- Ziploc freezer bag
- Tampons and/or sanitary napkins (make great bandages for wounds)
- Pepper spray for self-defense
- Prescription medications you might require
- Good map of area

Horse Trail Riding Safety and Etiquette

- Hoof pick
- Leather punch / tack repair kit
- Reflective tape
- Extra rope and/or baling twine
- Sponge – other items in which to cool your horse (water/alcohol or witch hazel mixes)

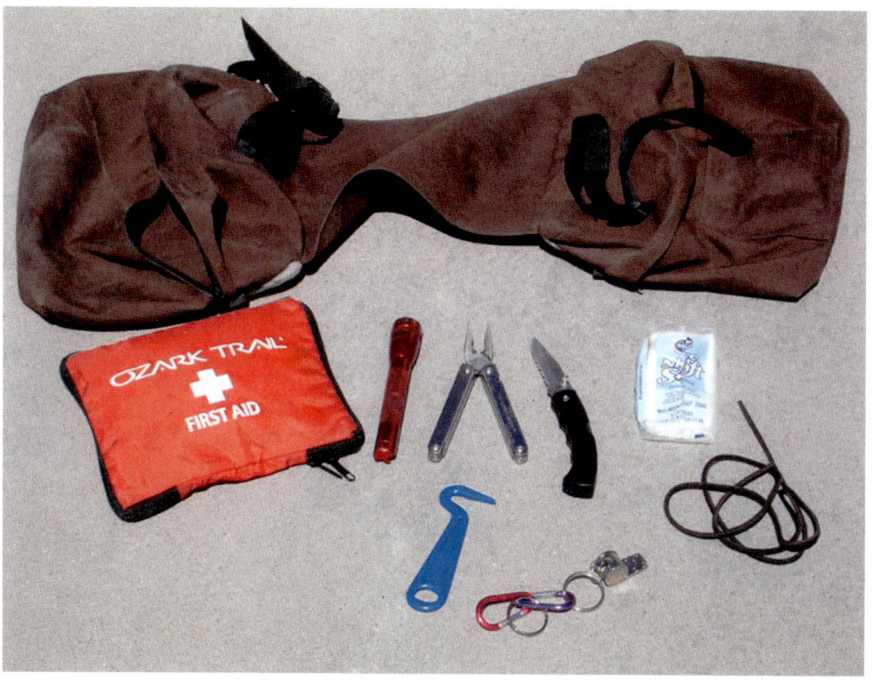

Must have items for your saddle bags.
Photo by Kim Baker

3 BAD WEATHER

Follow these simple steps when bad weather threatens your trail ride:

Be Prepared
Before you head out on the trail check the weather reports so you know what is forecasted for the day. If thunderstorms are possible later in the day, then ride in the morning hours. If a big storm is coming in, perhaps it's best to wait for a better day to ride, or stick close to home so you can cut the ride short at the first sign of bad weather. Dress in layers and have all of your safety gear with you (see Checklist).

Stay Calm
If you do get caught in a storm, it's best to try to seek some shelter and just wait it out rather than trying to ride it out. Elements like lightning and hail are likely to spook even the most well mannered, trained trail horses. Do your best to keep your horse calm, but your first priority should be to protect yourself. If you need to let go of your horse or if your horse gets away from you, do not panic. Protect yourself until the storm passes, then look for your horse. If you cannot find your horse relatively quickly, head for home or back to the trailer and call for help.

Here are some tips on what to do in specific types of bad weather. Remember to protect yourself first, then your horse.

Thunderstorm
If you are caught in a thunderstorm you can count the number of seconds between a lightning strike and a rumble of thunder. The closer they are

together, the closer the storm is to your location. At the first sound of thunder or sight of lightning, turn around and immediately head home or back to the trailer, because you and your horse are in danger. If the time between the lightning strike and rumble of thunder is less than 50 seconds, dismount your horse and seek shelter immediately. It takes five seconds for sound to travel one mile. Thus, 50 seconds equals 10 miles. Lightning can strike 10-15 miles away from the rain portion of the thunderstorm.

Lightning

Lightning is very dangerous and can be fatal to you and your horse. More humans survive lightning strikes than horses do. Lightning will strike the tallest object around; therefore, you need to dismount your horse immediately. Do NOT seek shelter under a tree. If lightning strikes the tree, parts of or the entire tree will explode and you and your horse will be impacted by debris. Seek a low lying area and crouch down, tuck your head and cover your ears. Loosely tie your horse (in case he needs to get free to protect himself) to a bush and move a safe distance away to protect yourself.

Hailstorm

Seek shelter immediately. Keep your helmet/hat on to protect your head. Keep the saddle on to protect your horse's back. If you cannot find shelter keep your back and your horse's back toward the direction the hail is falling. Get your horse to lower his head if possible to try to protect his head.

Sand/Dust/Wind Storm

Seek shelter immediately or get behind something solid. Keep your back and your horse's back toward the direction of the storm to protect your eyes.

Flash Flood

You might be out of the storm's path or never even see the storm, but that doesn't mean you couldn't be caught off guard by a flash flood. If you checked the weather reports and know storms are possible and you're riding in an area prone to flash floods, stay on high ground or avoid that area for the day. Flash floods can overtake you within a matter of seconds. Always seek higher ground as quickly as possible.

KIM BAKER

Colorado Thunderstorm
Photo by Mike Baker

4 TRAILER CHECKLIST

Before you hook up your trailer to head out on the trails, make sure your trailer is in proper working order. Review this check list before you haul out:

- Check all the working parts of your trailer like door, ramp and window hinges, as well as your jack stand gear box to make sure they move freely…oil/grease as needed.
- Check air pressure in tires.
- Check tires for wear (remember the spare, too!), and look for weather cracking; replace any tires that show these signs.
- Check wheel bearings and grease as needed.
- Check all electrical wires for damage.
- Check all lights, turn signals and brake lights to ensure they are working properly.
- Check the emergency brake to make sure it's working.
- Check window screens for any damage and repair as needed.
- Check all the mats and replace any that are torn or worn down.
- Check flooring for rotten areas or weak spots and replace immediately.
- Check coupler and ensure all parts are in working order.
- Check safety chains for any weak spots and replace immediately.
- Open doors and windows to allow trailer to air out.
- Put in fresh shavings if you use them.
- Check trailer ties to ensure the quick release snaps are working properly and the tie itself is not torn or worn. Replace as needed.
- If you have a water tank, fill it with fresh water.

- Check roof and side walls for any water leaks, seal as necessary.

Before you load your horse, hook up your trailer and take it for a short test drive. Ask a friend or spouse to come along or drive while you watch the motion and function of your trailer to ensure everything is in proper working order.

It's better to be safe than sorry, especially when hauling your best friend.

Horse Trailer
Photo by Kim Baker

5 KEEPING YOUR HORSE COOL IN HOT WEATHER

To keep your horse cool while riding during the hot summer months, consider these tips:

Ride Times
Avoid the hottest part of the day by riding early in the morning or in the late evenings. Refrain from overloading your horse with heavy saddlebags; take just what you need to stay safe and cool. Horse boots increase heat, so leave them off, or if you must ride with them make sure they are the last thing you put on your horse and the first thing you take off; do not leave them on your horse for extended periods.

Traveling
Open all windows and vents on your trailer, but do not allow your horse's head to extend outside the window. Remove fly sheets or blankets. Use lighter shipping boots, or go with as minimal protection as possible; perhaps just some leg wraps or bell boots. A trailer can easily be 20 degrees hotter than the outside air temperature, and horses working to maintain their balance during the trip can quickly become overheated, stressed and fatigued. Have some water on board to offer your horse during breaks on your trip, and once you reach your destination. If you're traveling long distances, stop every 4 hours for at least 30 minutes to give your horse a break and offer him some water. If possible, park in a shady place. Try not to travel during the hottest part of the day.

Arrival at Destination
Once you have arrived, unload your horse as soon as you have a safe place to keep him and offer him water. Keep an eye on how much water your horse is drinking by monitoring the water level in the bucket or trough and/or do the capillary refill or pinched skin test. Information on horse vital signs and how to perform these tests is available here:
http://www.equusite.com/articles/health/healthVitalSigns.shtml

Hydration
Allow your horse to drink as much water as he wants, both at home and out on the trail. When you know your horse will be working hard during the heat, you can add electrolytes to his water before, during, and after those sessions. Veterinarians typically recommend adding the electrolytes a few days prior so your horse has time to adjust. In the event your horse doesn't like the taste of the electrolytes, also offer plain water. Apple juice added to your horse's water may encourage him to drink the "strange" water during your trip. Allow your horse to eat grass out on the trail because the grass contains moisture.

Cooling Off
The fastest way to cool your horse is to remove all tack and douse his neck with cold water. If you're close to home or at the barn, a hose is the best option. Out on the trail, endurance riders dip sponges tied on their saddles with long strings into cool streams to water their horse's necks. If you won't be riding near a stream, carry an alcohol/water mix solution in your saddle bag and sponge that on your horse's neck to cool him off.

Be Fit
Most importantly, keep your horse fit. A fit horse will recover more quickly than an overweight horse. If your horse is overweight, establish a conditioning program that builds him up slowly to avoid injury and overheating.

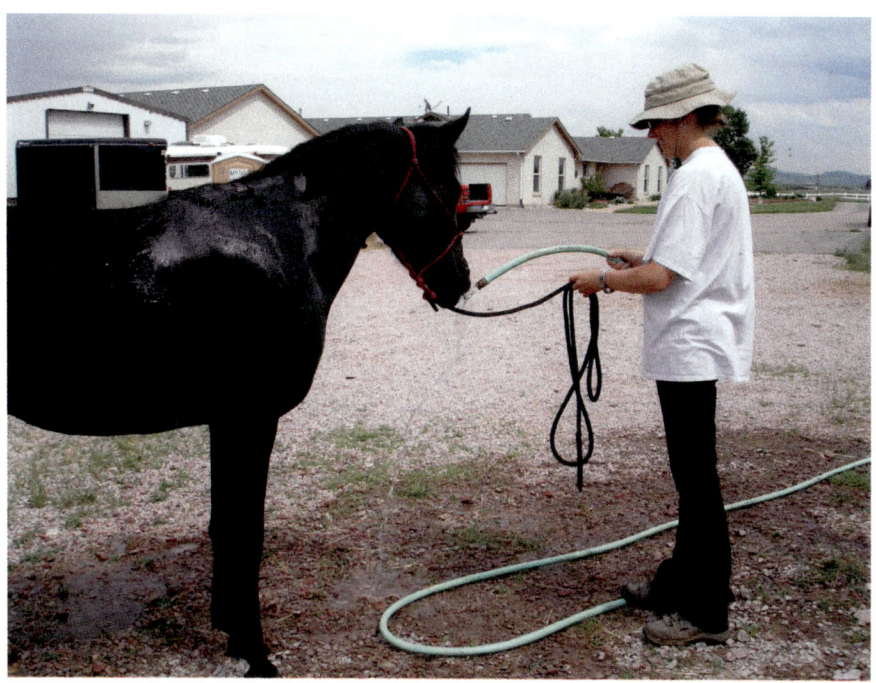

After cooling off the neck and shoulder, this horse also wanted a drink out of the hose.
Photo by Bernadette Spillane

6 HOW TO TELL IF YOUR HORSE IS OVERHEATED

Warning signs of heat stress in your horse include:

- Elevated breathing. More than 40-50 breaths per minute in an inactive horse, or after several minutes rest (2-5 minutes) your horse's breathing doesn't return to normal. Normal range is 4-16 breaths per minute.
- Elevated heart rate. More than 80 beats per minute in an inactive horse, or after several minutes rest (2-5 minutes) your horse's heart rate doesn't return to normal, or it climbs after rest. Normal range is 40-50 beats per minute at rest.
- Profuse sweating or no sweat at all.
- Elevated temperature. More than 103-105 degrees. Normal range is 99-101.
- Lethargy and/or depressed attitude. Doesn't want to move, doesn't want to eat, or becomes disinterested.
- Dehydration. Flanks are caved in, pinch test of the skin on the neck doesn't snap back quickly, and/or the mucous membranes are discolored (specifically a dark red, purple or "muddy" color). Normal is pink colored.

What to do when you recognize any or all of these signs:

1. Stop what you are doing and call your veterinarian, especially if the signs do not improve within 10 minutes.

Horse Trail Riding Safety and Etiquette

2. Remove all tack.
3. Douse your horse with cold water.
4. Find shade.
5. Seek a breeze, either natural or with a fan.
6. Offer water to drink.
7. Wait for your veterinarian to arrive.

7 PRE-RIDE CHECKLIST

Being well prepared before each ride ensures you and your horse have a safe and fun ride.

Tack
- Saddle fits properly
- Saddle is in good condition (leather is not cracked or worn)
- Saddle is adjusted correctly (not too tight or too loose)
- Bridle fits properly
- Bridle is in good condition (leather is not cracked or worn)
- Bridle is adjusted correctly (0-2 wrinkles in the corner of the mouth)

Horse
- Physical condition
    - Groomed
    - Hooves picked out
    - No swelling or strange bumps
    - Moving soundly (not lame)
- What kind of mood is your horse in?
    - Do some ground exercises to find out.
- Is your horse listening to you?
    - Do some ground exercises to find out.

Horses can have good days and bad days just like us. They can be distracted or irritable. If we take the time to find out how they are doing today, then we can set ourselves up for a safe, productive and happy ride. In some cases, it might be best to put up your horse and ride on a better day.

Rider
- Physical condition
    - Able to ride
    - Dressed to ride
- What kind of mood are you in?
    - Are you angry, irritable, distracted or flustered?
        - * Sometimes we need to set up our mental state and become prepared to ride. If we're distracted by something else, we are not focused on our horse and could end up injuring ourselves, our horse, or just have an unproductive/miserable ride.
- Are you listening to your horse?
    - Horses are talking to us all the time with their body language. The point is, are you listening? Are you in tune with your horse and what his or her body language is telling you?

It's important to be well prepared for any ride, whether out on the trail, or just a training session in an arena. If horse and rider are tuned in to each other, they can accomplish far more than when they are at odds with each other. If either partner is not feeling well, that makes it harder to do their job. So take it in stride, ride for a shorter period, or don't ride at all that day until both parties are 100% up to the job physically and emotionally.

Horse and rider have completed their pre-ride checklist and are ready to hit the trail.
Photo by Carla Diana

8 HUNTING SEASON

Fall is a wonderful time of year to ride with the cooler air, rich colors, and just being outside enjoying nature with your equine friend. Hunting season coincides with fall, so be prepared before you step out the door.

Bright Colors for You and Your Horse
Wearing bright colors ensures visibility for you and your horse. You can purchase bright orange hunting vests at any sporting-goods store. Some vests are reversible so you can wear them during other seasons as well. Bright yellow is also an option, like cross-walk guards; they include reflective tape in case you're out during dawn and/or dusk when visibility is low. Don't forget to outfit your horse in brightly colored gear as well. You don't want your horse to be mistaken for deer or elk. Outfit your horse in a brightly colored halter under your bridle, and use brightly colored saddle bags. Tie brightly colored ribbons in his mane and tail.

Determine a Location to Ride
Contact the Division of Wildlife or other Game Administration to determine the dates of different hunting seasons, and the locations where the hunting is allowed to take place. Plan to ride in areas that are less concentrated with hunters. If possible try riding out in the open, where visibility is high. If you do break for lunch or bio-needs, make sure you tie your horse in an open area or meadow where visibility is high.

Prepare Your Horse
Bird hunting is typically done with bird shot, compared to bow hunting, or long distance rifles for bigger game. Long distance rifles are the most

dangerous, the loudest and most likely to scare your horse. Train your horse to tolerate gunfire. You can start at home, or if you live near neighbors who shoot you can ask for their assistance. A cap pistol is a good place start, then upgrade to a starting pistol. As with any gun, exhibit gun safety for yourself and your horse. Never point a gun at another person or your horse. If guns are not your thing, try a bull-whip or enlist a friend who has bull-whip experience. The loud crack of bull-whip is an excellent way to desensitize your horse to loud noises. Of course we cannot prepare our horse for every possible situation, so expect your horse to be a little unsettled out on the trail with loud gunfire. Remember to remain calm and use your one-rein stop and emergency dismount if necessary. The less you worry and relax the more calm your horse will be.

Safety
Fall riding is the perfect time to practice and utilize trail safety. Ride with a buddy. Wear layered clothing and safety gear, and carry first aid kits. Stay on designated trails. Hunting season is not the time to be bushwhacking through the forest. It's also best to leave your dog at home, so he doesn't mix with a hunter's bird dog or get mistaken for a coyote.

Etiquette
Stay with your fellow riders. Be courteous to others out on the trail, including hunters. If you come upon a hunter's camp, announce yourself and don't just ride through their camp as if you own the place. Know that the hunters have a right to be there, even if you do not agree with their purpose. They do pay to be on the land and for the activity they are doing.

These riders are riding in the middle of the day to avoid hunters, but they still have bright visible clothing and tack on their horses. Check out the bright colored halters and breast collars.
Photo by Kim Baker

9 DOGS

Many horse owners are also dog owners, but that doesn't mean horses and dogs always mix well together. If you're out trail riding and a dog comes out of nowhere charging at your horse; do you know what to do?

Practice, practice, practice at home. Your horse should willingly stop, back and go forward with light body and verbal cues.

A moving target is difficult for a dog or any animal to make a connection. If the dog comes from behind, move your horse so he is facing the dog. If necessary, keep moving your horse's hips around to prevent the dog from making contact with your horse. Always move the hind end away from the dog so the horse is facing the dog. If your horse wants to strike out at the dog, allow him to do so if the dog is extremely aggressive. Sometimes this will get the dog to back off. If you feel confident and your horse is confident you can also charge after the dog. If the terrain is good and you're comfortable, you can canter off in an attempt to outrun the dog. Your confidence and your horse's confidence are important for this maneuver as you'll need to be able to direct your horse and get him to stop when safely out of reach of the dog.

The main goal here is your safety first, then your horse's safety. In scary situations pulling back on both reins will cause your horse to explode and possibly dump you. Using only one rein (straight up), turning onto a circle, and moving your horse's hips over are great ways to redirect your horse's nervous energy.

Loose dogs running free out on the trail.
Photo by Jennifer Tatnall

10 BIKES

The majority of equestrian trails are multi-use. This means we share trails with hikers, bikers and other users. Most of us have probably been startled by a biker out on the trail. Bikers are relatively quiet and they can move fast, especially downhill. Plus, a lot of trails have blind corners. The sudden appearance of a fast moving object can scare even the most well-mannered trail horse. The following tips will help you prepare to expect the unexpected out on the trail.

Introduce the bike from the ground
Invite a friend to come over with her bike. Allow your horse to walk up to and smell the bike. Once your horse is comfortable with the bike at a standstill, ask your friend to start to move the bike slowly. Have your friend move the bike away from your horse while you and your horse follow the bike. When your horse is comfortable with the bike moving away from him, ask your friend to move the bike back and forth in front of him. If your horse needs to move his feet, that's ok, allow him to do so, but always ask him to face the bike. Eventually he will become comfortable with the bike moving in front of him and he will stand still as the bike moves. Allow your horse the time he needs to get used to the bike. This may happen in one session or several. Reward your horse for exploring the bike and remaining calm.

Mounted

Now that your horse accepts the bike from the ground, ask your friend to mount the bike and ride slowly away from your horse while you and your horse follow. Repeat the same steps from above, while you remain on the ground and your friend rides the bike. When your horse is comfortable with the mounted biker, you can mount up, too, and interact. Start by following the biker, then have the biker go back and forth in front of you and your horse, eventually working up to the biker approaching your horse both head on and from behind. Work with your friend announcing herself and not announcing (a surprise) from behind your horse. The more you can expose your horse to different scenarios the better prepared you both will be out on the trail. Get creative with it, and have fun.

Etiquette

You and your horse are ambassadors for other trail riders. Always be courteous to others out on the trail, even if they are not courteous to you. Whenever possible and safe to do so, pull off the trail and allow the biker(s) to go by. Have your horse turn and face the biker(s). Announce yourself if you are coming up on a group of hikers or bikers. When passing or being passed, announce how many riders you have in your group. If your horse is really jumpy around bikers, ask the bikers to dismount and walk their bikes slowly past you. The friendlier you are and the more information you provide, the better the experience for everyone out on the trail. A lot of people don't know what scares horses, so be courteous and ask them to help you out and explain why your horse is afraid. Always remember to say thank you!

Other Trail Users

Believe it or not, horses can spook at hikers with big backpacks. All of sudden what was just a human is now a large "thing" with something attached. Use the same technique described above for bikers to prepare your horse at home for backpackers. You can also ask the hiker to talk out loud so the horse knows it's another human.

ATVs are loud and fast moving. The best approach is to ride on trails not designated for ATV use; however, on many public lands or national forest, where ATVs are allowed, an encounter is likely. Use the same steps described above to help your horse accept ATVs. If you don't have an ATV you can use a lawn mower or garden tractor. Out on the trail, take a wide berth around the ATVs whenever possible and have your horse turn and face them as they pass by.

Mountain bikers can scare the most well-mannered trail horse.
Photo by Andy Fortna

11 SUMMARY

Trail riding can be an extremely rewarding experience for you and your horse, a chance to explore places of beauty and wonder created by nature. Rarely can you prepare for everything that may happen, but the more prepared you are, the better equipped you'll be to handle whatever transpires out on the trail. Don't underestimate practicing at home. Even taking short trips around the block from your barn is good experience and exposure for you and your horse. Before heading away from home, check the weather forecast, ensure your trailer is in good working order, and carry the necessary equipment for you and your horse to stay hydrated and comfortable out on the trail. Remember to be courteous to other trail users. If every equestrian encounter on the trail is courteous and pleasant, trails will always be open and available to us equestrians.

Happy and Safe Trail Riding!

ABOUT THE AUTHOR

Photo by Lisette Zandvort

An animal lover and healer, Kim Baker took her first pony ride at the age of four. She has several decades of understanding and knowledge in the ways of animals which drove her to seek a new career in horses and animals after being laid off from Corporate IT in 2006. She received her Bachelor of Science degree in Ecology and Evolutionary Biology from the University of Arizona in 1998, and later received her Master's Degree in Integrated Sciences [Biology, Mathematics, and Computer Science] from the University of Colorado at Denver in 2005.

Writing for local and national magazines, as well as international online information sites, Kim is also the radio host of the "Kim Baker Show, " an internet talk radio show about the amazing connection between horses, animals and humans. Visit www.kimbakershow.com to listen. She has fascinating guests, tips and advice from experts and so much more!

Kim Baker is also the founder of KB Natural Horsemanship: the most integrated horse and animal program available.
www.kbnaturalhorsemanship.com

Kim lives with her two dogs, two horses and a barn cat in Colorado.

WANT THE *ULTIMATE* RELATIONSHIP WITH YOUR HORSE?

Just like Kim has with Night?

Here's how you can get it!

Just 7 Steps to the Horse of Your Dreams

Lead your bucking, rearing, disrespectful horse to the relationship you've always dreamed of!

Echo was as wild as horses come. She would buck anyone or anything off! She also reared when she had a mind to. No one wanted her. She was passed from trainer to trainer with no improvement.

Finally one trainer took Echo on. With some dedication, patience, and following the 7 steps of "Groundwork Essentials," Echo turned into the DREAM HORSE for one young girl. The girl fell in love with Echo, and they rode off happily into the sunset.

Hi, I'm Kim Baker, and I'm the trainer that helped Echo find her forever friend. And now, whether you have a bucking bronco, or are just trying to deepen the connection you and your horse know is waiting for you, I can help.

My DVD program, "Groundwork Essentials" is designed to show you:

* How to regain your horse's TRUST.

* How to earn your horse's RESPECT.

* How to create a wide open channel of COMMUNICATION between you and your horse.

* How to develop a DEEPER, RICHER CONNECTION with your horse.

* How to avoid common mistakes horse owner make that DESTROY their relationship with their horse.

* And much more...

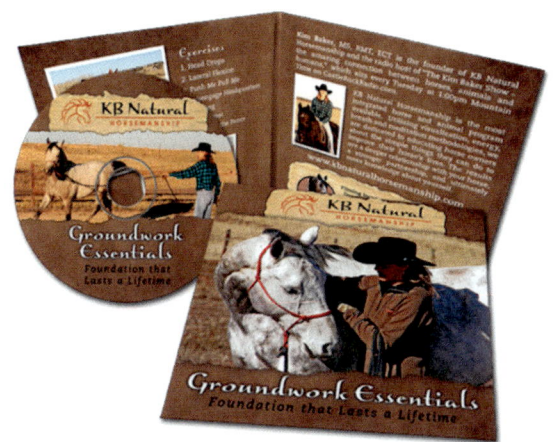

DON'T MISS OUT! Nearly 2 information-packed hours of POWERFUL information which will TRANSFORM your relationship with your horse to one you've only dreamed of!

GET YOUR COPY TODAY!!!

Only $34.97 (plus shipping and handling) *That's about what you'd pay for ONE meal out for a family of four!*

GET IT HERE: http://www.kbnaturalhorsemanship.com/shopping-corral/groundwork-essentials-dvd

STOP BEING AFRAID OF YOUR HORSE AND LEARN HOW TO CREATE THE RELATIONSHIP AND PARTNERSHIP YOU'VE ALWAYS DREAMED OF!

$1 FROM EVERY DVD GOES TO HAPPY DOG RANCH RESCUE 501C3 FOUNDATION TO SUPPORT ANIMALS IN NEED AND THAT PROVIDE THERAPY TO OTHERS.

Made in the USA
San Bernardino, CA
03 March 2020